Functional Recipes COOKBOOK

For Weight Loss / Diabetic / Hypertensive

HALA HAMZA SEIF

ISBN: Softcover   978-1-9845-6639-3
       Hardcover   978-1-9845-6640-9
       EBook   978-1-9845-6638-6

Print information available on the last page

Rev. date: 01/07/2018

To order additional copies of this book, contact:
Xlibris
1-888-795-4274
www.Xlibris.com
Orders@Xlibris.com

Dedication

With All my Love I dedicate my book

To the precious spirit of my mother who was my first love and the top of tenderness, sincerity and love. May God bless you and I hope to make you always proud of me and will remain your memory with my heart and soul forever my angel....

To the spirit of my beloved father who left us early but his memory and his love will remain forever

To my dear husband Hisham, childhood lover and now, my friend and my first supporter, may God keep you by my side and my heart for life...

To my children Hani, Hazar. Haidi You are a piece of my heart and my soul and my desire for success and giving, but to be the best role model for you in life, I wish you happiness and success and achieve your self and your purpose in life

To my beloved brothers and sisters, I love you all. You are a treasure in this world...

To all my friends, loved ones, my relatives and all those who loved me and supported me. They were the ray of light that lit my way and encouraged me to the best. I always wish you happiness and light in your life like what you shared with me....

I Love You All......

FUNCTIONAL RECIPES COOKBOOK

FOR WEIGHT LOSS /DIABETIC /HYPERTENSIVE/

EAT TASTY AND LIVE HEALTHY

EAT AND LOSE WEIGHT

The recipes in this book are healthy, delicious and easy to make. Most of the ingredients are specified as functional nutrients because of the effective role that they play in the human body, biological process from increasing the digesting system speed like the fibers and reducing the insulin resistance like cinnamon, which increase cells sensitivity to the insulin presence. And this will reduce the amount of insulin in the blood (since the insulin is the major factor to store the fat in the body especially in tummy and waist area) and by this way it will lead automatically to weight loss and more regular blood sugar. Plus a lot of herbs and spices that relax the vessels and the nerve system and reduce the water retention and help the body in drainage like cumin, ginger, anise spices, and garlic which have great effect in regulating the high blood pressure.

Beside the insulin regulator ingredients, the recipes has a plenty of Anti-oxidants (natural food color from chlorophyll), anthocyanin, that helps in detoxifying the body from different toxins that might accumulate from medicines and manufactured food and chemicals. And by this way, it will limit the free radicals production and protect the body from harm and some dangerous diseases like cancer, obesity, heart problems.

More over the antioxidants, the recipes has a lot of Omega three and Omega six and beneficial unsaturated fatty acid which will help in reducing the LDL (Bad cholesterol) and elevating the HDL (Good cholesterol), increasing the flexibility of the arteries and help to keep it open and prevent the block out so it will protect from heart attacks and strengthen the heart and vessels.

So, this is an example for what the functional recipes can help you in your daily life to have a better food style and educate your children and lovers on the correct way of choosing your food and a straight way to better health.

And even if you want to try to cook your favorite recipes, still you can do that for healthier and more beneficial food, because you are what you eat so eat well and stay well.

Here are some simple tips to do so ….

How to Modify Recipes to Reduce Fat and Calories (without losing the flavor!)

Eating healthy doesn't mean having to give up all your favorite foods. Unless you're on a specific diet or have some medical condition that requires you to seriously change your food intake. There are a lot of small things you can do to modify recipes on your own.

Here is a start on healthy substitutions*

Replace...
- Margarine/ butter (spread) <u>with</u> low-sugar preserves, fat-free cream cheese, fat free spray butter, Promise in the tub fat free or Butter Buds
- Regular cheese <u>with</u> low-fat or fat-free
- Regular salad <u>with</u> dressing Balsamic vinegar, low-fat salad dressing, lemon juice
- Whole dairy products (sour cream, milk, yogurt, etc.) <u>with</u> low-fat or fat-free dairy products
- Nuts <u>with</u> crunchy cereal nuggets (i.e. Grape Nuts, fat-free granola, crushed Corn Flakes)
- Chocolate chips <u>with</u> raisins

Replace...
- Regular Jell-O <u>with</u> sugar-free Jell-O
- Biscuits <u>with</u> low-fat corn muffins, or make your own whole wheat biscuits fat free
- Frying foods <u>with</u> grilling, poaching, steaming, stir-frying, roasting, microwaving, or red meat <u>with</u> legumes and lentils (partial substitutions are ok)
- Mayonnaise <u>with</u> mustard, salsa, or fat free mayonnaise
- Whole eggs <u>with</u> egg whites or egg substitute
- All-purpose flour <u>with</u> ½ of the flour total with whole wheat flour
- Solid fats <u>with</u> vegetable oils

—

- Salt. Reduce to a minimum or eliminate completely from most recipes.
- Butter or shortening. Most things can be cooked with non-stick spray.
- Sugar. Use vanilla extract or cinnamon to give the impression of sweetness.

Replace...

- Syrup. Most syrups are added after the dish is done, to increase flavour or better texture. Either replace with a sugar-free option or avoid completely.
- Mayonnaise. You can replace with low-fat mayo if you want, use oil-free dressings, or avoid completely.
- Egg Yolks. Unless you have a specific reason for leaving them in (such as coloring), use egg whites only, which contain no fat and no calories.

–

Modifying recipes makes eating healthfully delicious

Reduce fat
Replace half the oil, shortening or butter in baking with applesauce
Sauté in broth or water.
Use nonstick pans and cooking spray to keep food from sticking.

Reduce sodium
Salt can be reduced by one-half in most recipes.
Use no-salt-added canned goods and try frozen vegetables rather than canned. Rinse canned vegetables before adding to a recipe.

Reduce sugar
When cutting back on the amount of sugar in a recipe (reduce by one-quarter to one-third) try adding spices, such as vanilla or cinnamon to enhance flavor., and use the sweetener zero calorie.

Increase fiber
Substitute brown rice, barley, quinoa or other whole grains for white rice.
Replace half the white flour in a recipe with whole wheat flour.
Try whole grain pasta, rather than white pasta.
Add beans rather than meat to soups and stews. This reduces calories from fat, lowers costs and increases fiber.

Make your food tasty by adding functional and healthy spices.

Use always measuring cups and spoons especially for oil and sugar to limit the amount. Finally, cook with love to send your positive energy to your food. Love can regulate some glands and it will make your food tastier and very easy to be digested.

Contents

Functional Ingredients & Benefits

<u>Cinnamon</u> Regulates blood sugar and reduce insulin resistance and help in weight reduction and reduce PCOS symptoms, alkaline the blood and increase immunity.

<u>Turmeric</u> Anti-inflammatory, increase immunity and alkaline the blood and fight cancer and cholesterol

<u>Flax seeds</u> Reduce the bad cholesterol LDL and increase the good cholesterol HDL, and reduce the triglyceride and help in appetite suppression and weight loss and increase the inner satisfaction and improve the mental health and treat constipation, alkaline the blood and increase immunity.

<u>Chia Seeds</u> High source of protein, regulate the blood pressure and sugar it is great for weight loss and constipation and PCOS symptoms, alkaline the blood and increase immunity.

<u>Buckwheat</u> Great source of free gluten carbs for people with allergy to gluten product and high protein and fiber carbs, which not elevate the blood sugar so fast, and great for diabetics and hypertensive and for weight reduction seekers. Alkaline the blood and increase immunity.

<u>Quinoa</u> Great source of protein and healthy carbs and fibers great for Diabetics, regulate high blood pressure, help in weight loss and appetite suppression and PCOS Symptoms. Alkaline the blood and increase immunity.

<u>Stevia Sugar</u> Great Natural Sweetener Suitable to give the high sweet test with lowest possible calories without elevating blood sugar and insulin very fast and still keep the blood not so far from alkalinity .so it is the best sweetener for Diabetic,high Cholesterol and cardiac disease patients.

<u>Coconut Oil</u> The healthiest cooking oil for all kind of health problem for people with high cholesterol, and diabetics, help in weight loss, and regulate the blood pressure, plus improving the health of Hear and Skin and Nails with the group of Vitamin K,E,D,A.

<u>Almond Flour</u> High in Protein and rich in Fibers and Anti-Oxidants and Omega 3 and Omega 6 which makes it great for high cholesterol, blood sugar and pressure, weight loss,and for hair and skin and nail.as well as mental health.

<u>Oat Bran</u> Great source of high quality fibers, rich in Vitamin B, reduces blood sugar and pressure, and reduce weight and reduce the fat percentage in the body composition plus treat constipation.

<u>Anise Spices, Paprika</u> Anti-oxidants and anti-inflammatory, reduce the free radical, regulate blood sugar and help for better sleep and relaxation.

<u>Olive Oil</u> Reduce the LDL and increase the good cholesterol HDL and help in increasing the Arteries elasticity and strengthen the Health of the heart and hair and skin, treat slow digestion and constipation.

<u>Brown Rice</u> Great for regulating the blood pressure and sugar and helps in weight loss and increase the digestive and improve the serotonin production and improve the mental health.

<u>Garlic & Onion, Ginger</u> They are great for cardiac problems, it helps in opening the arteries and reduce the bad cholesterol, the LDL and increase the good cholesterol the HDL, decrease the blood pressure, regulate the blood sugar, anti-inflammatory, anti-oxidants decrease the free radical, increase immunity and Alkaline the blood, Detoxify the body, increase the digestion and decrease the water retention and the fat weight as well .fight cancers and Kidney Problems.

<u>Lemon juice</u> Great to reduce the blood pressure and help in preventing the kidney stone formulation, if you suffer from kidney stone, just take half lemon as a juice everyday, and the stone will be gone after a while if it is in the small size.

Breakfast

Hala Hamza Seif

Oat Bread with flax seeds

Category	Breakfast
Serving	8 pcs+8 balls of Labneh
Serving Size	1 pc Bread+1 Labneh Ball

Total breakfast calories   160 kcal/1 serve
Total kcal/ 1 pc 35 kcal for bread +100 for 1 Labneh balls

Cooking Items

1.5 cup	Oat Blend it as fine Flour
1 tbsp	Oil
0.2 tsp	Salt
1 tsp	Yeast
2 cup	Water
1.5 cup	Oat bran (blend it as powder)
1 tbsp	Flax seeds mill (Powder)
2 cup	Leafy vegetable
2 lit	Skim Yogurt

How to prepare:

Oat Bread: Mix the yeast with the warm water and leave it for 10 minutes. Mix all ingredients and half amount of oil together except the yogurt, then leave it to rest for at least 30 minutes.

Cut the dough into small balls, put little oil on your hands and roll the bread ball into slices then cook it in a non-sticky pan for 5 minutes each then turn the bread into other side and cook it for 5 minutes. Then serve it with Labneh ball and vegetable.

How to prepare Labneh: Put the yogurt on a clean cotton cloth that fixed over a colander for about 10 to 24 hours. Close the cloth and put a 1 kg weight over it until it become a dough. Throw the water that came from it and roll it as balls and save it in olive oil. You can add 1 tsp of salt and preferably not.

Arabic Bread

Category	Carbs/breakfast/lunch/dinner
Serving	6 pcs.

Total kcal/ 1 pc 50 kcal

Cooking Items

1 cup	Wheat Flour
⅛ tsp	Salt
1 tsp	Yeast
½ cup	Water
¼ cup	Flour no. 1 for rolling of dough
1 tsp	Sugar

How to prepare:

Mix all the yeast, sugar, water, and salt in a bowl. Make sure it's mix very well and leave it to rest for 10 minutes.

Then mix the liquid ingredients with flour and leave it for 30 minutes. Cover it all with plastic wrap.

After resting the dough, put some flour no.1 on the table and cut it to balls and roll it to circle then cover it with a clean cotton towel. Leave it for 1 hour.

Put in oven for 15-20 min in 200°C.

Oat Bran and Almond Bread

(for weight loss and diabetics)

Category	Breakfast / Dinner/Lunch
Serving	16 serving
Serving Size	1 pc

Total kcal/ 1 serve   85 kcal

Note: 6cm x 8cm the size of the bread

Cooking Items

2 cup	Whole almond Flour
1 tbsp	Olive Oil
1/8 tsp	Salt
1 tbsp	Yeast
1 cup	Water
2 cup	Oat bran
2 Pc	Egg
1 tsp	Black seeds
1 tsp	Sesame seeds
1 tsp	Flax seeds
1 tsp	Oregano
1 tsp	Garlic powder
1 tbsp	Wheat Flour
1 tsp	Baking powder
1 cup	Low fat milk or yogurt

How to prepare:

Mix the oat bran, almond flour, yeast, water, milk, baking powder, egg, salt in a bowl, make sure its mix very well.

Let the dough rest for 30 minutes. Cover it well with plastic wrap.

After resting the dough, put the olive oil in oven try and spread it well. Then spread the wheat flour and add the mixture and arrange it in the try then, spread the sesame seeds and flax seeds, oregano, garlic powder, black seeds on top of the try and over it with plastic wrap then leave it for 1 hour.

Bake it for 10-15 min at 450 F. Let it cool for 1 hour and cut it into square.

Hummus (chickpeas) w/ sesame Tahina

Category   Breakfast
Serving   3 serving
Serving Size   ½ cup

Total kcal/ 1 serve 200 kcal

Cooking Items

1 cup	Chickpeas (Hummus)
50 gm	Sesame Tahina
50 ml	Lemon juice
½ tsp	Salt
1 tsp	Olive oil
1 pc	Garlic
0.5 tsp	Paprika
0.5 tsp	Cumin powder

How to prepare:

Soak the chickpeas overnight.

Boil it in pressure cooker for 1 hr.

Blend the chickpeas (hummus) then add the tahina, smashed garlic, salt & lemon juice. Blend it well. Put it in the fridge to cool.

Pour it in container & put paprika and cumin and olive oil on the top if wanted.

Lunch

Beef Kofta with Grilled potato

Category	Lunch
Serving	12
Serving Size	1 Pc/Hand palm size

Total kcal 260 kcal/1 serve

Cooking Items

1 kg	Very Lean Beef meat
500 gm	Sweet or normal Potato
300 gm	Tomato
1 cup	Minced Parsley
50 gm	Yellow Capsicum
50 gm	Red Capsicum
50 gm	Green Capsicum
2 tsp	Salt for meat
1 tsp	Cinnamon
1 tsp	Paprika
1 tsp	Black pepper
100 gm	Onion
1 tbsp	Olive oil

How to prepare:

Peel and cut the potato into half-moon slices. Marinate it with the olive oil and bake it in the oven for 15 min from down at 450 F then for 3 min on broil from up and set it in the bottom of the tray.

Peel and wash the onion and put it in the blender or mixer with the capsicum and spices and blend it but do not make it juicy keep it as it is chopped in fine way. Then add the meat and all spices and salt and mix it will. Place it as a layer on top of the grilled potato.

Add the tomato slices on top of the meat and cover it with foil and bake it for 30 min on a 400 F. After that, remove the foil and broil it from up for 5 to 10 min. Then throw the fat that came out from it and cut it as squares and serve it with salad and yogurt sause.

Grilled Chicken Beryani

Category   Lunch
Serving   10 serving
Serving Size   ½ cup of rice
+100 gm chicken breast

Total kcal 325 kcal per serving

Cooking Items for Chicken

5 gm	Cardamom powder
3 gm	Black pepper
5 gm	Paprika(red pepper)
5 gm	Turmeric powder
15 gm	Salt
50 gm	Onion
10 gm	Garlic
30 gm	Tomato paste
15 gm	Shredded Ginger
1 kg	Chicken breast (cubes)
3 pc	Green bay leaves
5 gm	Cinnamon powder
5 gm	Coriander
100 gm	Green pepper

Cooking Items for Rice

2 cup	basmati rice (long grain)
4 cup	Water
1 tsp	Turmeric
50 gm	Raisin
100 gm	Onion
5 gm	Shredded Ginger
3 gm	Cardamom
3 gm	Glove grain
5 gm	Cinnamon
10 gm	Salt

How to prepare:

Chicken: Marinate the chicken with all ingredients in the chicken cooking items and leave it for 5 hours or 1 day, but inside the fridge.

Then the next day, place the chicken in the oven and cover it with foil then grill it at 400 F for 30 to 40 min. After it is cooked, remove the foil and let it be on broil to be golden from top.

In the meanwhile, place the water of the rice with all ingredients required for cooking the rice and when the water boils add the rice and keep the fire high for 10 min at least then cover the rice and reduce the fire for another 10 min to let the rice cook.

Serve the rice with the chicken and serve green salad beside them.

Optional: Decorate with oven roasted nuts and coriander.

Egg with Yellow Yogurt

Category   Lunch
Serving   5 Serving
Serving Size   1 cup of yogurt + 1 eggs + ½ cup of rice

Total calories   300 kcal
Total kcal/ per serving 300 kcal

Cooking Items

5 Eggs	Egg
1 lit	Low fat Yogurt
1 tsp	Corn flour
1.5 cup	Sushi rice
1 tsp	Salt
1 tsp	Turmeric
1 tsp	Salt for the rice
3 cup	Water

How to prepare:

Put the low fat yogurt in the mixer with the salt and turmeric and corn flour and mix it well. Then put it in a pan on medium fire and keep stirring till boiling for about 20 min.

When it boils, add the egg one by one and stop stirring. Leave it for 10 to 15 min to be cooked.

Soak the sushi rice for around 1 hour and boil it with water and salt on high fire then when it boils after 5 min reduce the fire till cook. Serve it hot with the egg with yogurt.

Grilled Chicken with Potato

Category	Lunch
Serving	3 Serving
Serving Size	1 Pc chicken +5 potato slices
Total kcal/ 1 serve	250 kcal

Cooking Items

300 gm	Potato
3 Slice	500 gm Chicken breast
3 pc	Garlic
1 tbsp	Oregano
1 tbsp	Rosemary
1 tbsp	Olive oil
1 tsp	Paprika
1 tsp	Cinnamon
7 gm	Salt
1 tbsp	Shredded Green Ginger
30 ml	Lemon juice

How to prepare:

Wash the chicken breast and cut it into 3 slices. Marinate it with ginger, smashed garlic, lemon juice and spices keep it for 3 hours at least in the fridge. Then peel and wash the potato and cut it into circle slices then put it in an oven tray and put the marinated chicken on top. Add the olive oil after and mix them well, cover it with foil and bake it for 15 -20 min. Then when it is cooked put it on a broil to give her the golden color from up, then serve it with boiled rice and green leafy salad.

Meat Pastry (Safiha)

Category	Lunch/dinner
Serving	10 Serving
Serving Size	1 pc
Total kcal/ 1 serve	160 kcal

Cooking Items for Meat Mixture

500 gm	Minced Beef
50 gm	Pomegranate sauce
1 tsp	Salt
100 gm	Green capsicum
5 gm	Black pepper
100 gm	Red capsicum
100 gm	Onion
100 gm	Tomato
1 tsp	Paprika
1 tsp	Cinnamon

For the Dough

4 cup	Whole wheat flour
0.5 tsp	salt
1 tsp	yeast
2 cup	water

How to prepare:

Dough:

Put the yeast in half cup warm water and mix it well then keep it for 10 min. Add the rest of water and salt and flour, mix it till become a nice dough and cover it with plastic wrap then keep it to rest in warm area for 1 hour.

Meat mixture:

Put the tomato, capsicums, onion, salt, spices pomegranate sauce in the blender mix it to be like smoothie then add the meat and mix it well.

Preparation:

Divide the dough into small balls and roll it to be a thin circle sheet, then add around 2 tbsp of meat mixture and spread it on top of the dough. Bake it for 7 min on 450 F from down only. Then serve it hot with salad.

Chicken Shawarma

Category	Lunch/dinner
Serving	2 serving
Serving Size	1 Sandwich (1 tortilla bread)
Total kcal/ 1 serve	270

How to prepare:

Wash the chicken and cut it into thin slices then marinate it with garlic, spices, olive oil, and grounded ginger paste. Leave it in the fridge overnight.

Put the mixed ingredients in a pan and cook it on a very low fire.

Put the cooked chicken in the bread in the middle then spread the mayonnaise & pickles and roll it. Roast it in the oven or a grill for 5 min.

Put in container together w/ the decoration that you choose. It can be great with garlic sauce and low salt pickles and lettuce.

Cooking Items

	100 gm	Chicken breast
	10 gm	Lemon juice
	1 tsp	Salt
	0.5 tsp	Green ginger
	2 gm	Black pepper
	2 gm	Cardamon
	0.5 tsp	Garlic powder
	1/8 tsp	Olive Oil
	1 tsp	Paprika
	1 pc	Garlic
50 gm	1 pc	Pickles (organic)
58.5 2 Pc	45 gm	Whole grain tortilla Bread
24.7	1 tsp	Mayonnaise (garlic sauce)
11.1	10 gm	Green pepper beside the sandwich
	10 gm	Lettuce for decoration if wanted

Buckwheat

Category	Lunch
Serving	3 serving
Serving Size	½ cup

Note Total Kcal for 1 Serve = 170 kcal

How to prepare:

Boil the Buckwheat in the water for 10 minutes and then add the salt and spices. Decorate it with flax seeds, pumpkin seeds, and chia seeds.

Cooking Items

100 gm	Buckwheat
1 cup	Water
3 gm	Salt
1 tsp	Flax seeds
1 tsp	Chia seeds
1 tbsp	Pumpkin seeds
3 gm	Cinnamon
2 gm	Turmeric

Red and White Quinoa

Category	Lunch
Serving	3 serving
Serving Size	½ cup

Note Total Kcal for 1 Serve = 100 kcal

Cooking Items

100 cup	White Quinoa
2 cup	Water
4 gm	Salt
40 gm	For decoration Cabbage
100 gm	Red Quinoa
3 gm	Cinnamon
3 gm	Turmeric
30 gm	Walnut

How to prepare:

Boil the quinoa in hot water for 10 minutes and remove the extra water. Add the spices and salt then decorate it with walnut and white and red cabbage.

Asparagus Sauté

Category	Lunch
Serving	5 serving
Serving Size	1 cup
Total kcal/ 1 serve	180 kcal

Cooking Items

800 gm	Asparagus
1 cup	Fresh Coriander
8 Pc	Garlic
2 tbsp	Olive Oil
2 tsp	Salt
1 tsp	Black pepper
1 tsp	Cinnamon
¼ cup	Lemon juice

How to prepare:

Cut the asparagus into 3-5 cm pieces and wash it. Cut half amount of garlic and sauté it with the olive oil for 5 minutes, then add the asparagus and sauté it and keep it an low fire for 10-15 minutes. When it is cooked, add the rest smashed garlic and the coriander with the rest of spices, then add the lemon juice and serve it with healthy bread.

Broccoli Curry

Category	Lunch
Serving	5 serving
Serving Size	1 cup

Total kcal/ 1 serve 200 kcal

100 gm	Onion
50 ml	Yogurt
100 ml	Light sour cream

Cooking Items

800 gm	Broccoli
200 gm	Tomato
4 Pc	Garlic
1 tbsp	Olive Oil
2 tsp	Salt
1 tsp	Green Ginger
2 cup	Water
1 tsp	Cinnamon
¼ cup	Coriander
1 tsp	Turmeric powder
1 tsp	Curry spices
100 gm	Green pepper

How to prepare:

Wash the broccoli, cut it to small pieces, and steam it for 5 to 10 minutes.

To make the curry sauce, cut the onion into cubes and sauté it with oil for 5 minutes then add the smashed garlic, shredded ginger, cubes of green pepper and tomato, and water. Let it boil with the water then add the salt, turmeric, cinnamon, curry spices, and half amount of the sour cream. Let it boil for 5 minutes then add the steamed broccoli. For decoration, add the remaining of sour cream to the yogurt and decorate the broccoli curry and spread the fresh coriander on top. Serve it with brown rice or healthy bread.

Hala Hamza Seif

Green Beans with Tomato

Category	Lunch
Serving	5 serving
Serving Size	1 cup
Total kcal/ 1 serve	170 kcal

Cooking Items

800 gm	Green beans
400 gm	Tomato
8 Pc	Garlic
2 tbsp	Olive Oil
2 tsp	Salt
1 tsp	Cinnamon
2.5 cup	Water
1 tsp	Paprika
100 gm	Onion

How to prepare:

Cut the green beans into smaller pieces with length of 3-5 cm and wash it well.

Sauté the cubes of onion and the half amount of peeled garlic with olive oil for 5 minutes then add the green beans. Leave it on low fire until it is cooked for about 20 minutes.

Peel the tomato, cut very small, smash the garlic and add them to the beans.

Cook it for 10 min and add the salt and spices.

After cooled, pour it in the container. Serve it with the almond with oat bran bread.

Millet with Vegetable

Category	Lunch
Serving	3 serving
Serving Size	1 cup

Total kcal per serving 125 kcal

Note: This meal is perfect for insulin resistant, and for diabetic as of.

Shopping	Cooking	Food Item
85 gm	½ cup	Millet seeds
2.5 ml	½ tsp	Garlic
125 ml	½ cup	Water
1.25 gm	¼ tsp	Salt
1.25 gm	¼ tsp	Paprika
1.25 gm	¼ tsp	Turmeric
	1 tsp	Flax seeds

	1 tsp	Chia Seeds
	30 gm	White Cabbage
	30 gm	Red Cabbage
0.5 pc	30 gm	Onion
0.5 pc	30 gm	Carrot
	3 cup	Water

Cooking Items

Cut all vegetables into thin long slices. Put the water in the pan and add the millet seeds, vegetables, boil them on medium fire for almost 10-15 minutes.

When the seeds are cooked, sieve the extra water then put the cooked millet in the plate and add the salt, paprika, turmeric, and mix them. Arrange them in a good way and spread the flax seeds and chia seeds on top of them.

Stuffed Grape Leaves with Vegetables

Category	Dinner
Serving	15 serving
Serving Size	6-7 pcs
Total kcal/ 1 serve	130 kcal

Cooking Items

500 gm	1 Big bundle	parsley
300 gm	½ Big bundle	Fresh mint
30 gm	5 Pcs	Green onion
500 gm	6 Pcs	Tomato
125 ml	½ cup	Lemon juice
10 gm	2 tsp	Salt (rice& water)
	½ tsp	Mix spices(seasoning spices)
	3 tbsp	Olive oil
	2 cup	Sushi rice
	1.25 Bottle	Grape leaves

How to prepare:

Soak the rice overnight. Then cook it. Cut tomato, green onion, parsley, and fresh mint finely. Mix it with rice and all other ingredients. Pour olive oil and lemon juice, salt, mix spices. Keep it aside for soaking.

Spread the wine leaves and put this rice mixture on the leaves and fold it nicely.

Arrange the stuffed Grape leaves inside the pan and add water up to cover.

Put one dish on the top of the Grape leaves and close the pan and cook it for 1 hour on medium fire.

Then add lemon juice and cook for another 1 hour.

Switch off the fire and keep it for cooling.

Grilled Fish Fillet with Herbs and Sauce

Category	Lunch with rice
Serving	6 serving
Serving Size	2 pc of fish fillet

Total kcal/ 1 serve 240 kcal

3 Pc	Garlic
½ cup	Lemon juice
1 tbsp	Sesame tahina
½ cup	Water

Cooking Items

800 gm	12 Pc	Fish fillet

For marinating

70 ml	¼ cup	Lemon juice
10 gm	2 tsp	Skin of Lemon
10 gm	3 Pc	Garlic
15 gm	1 tbsp	Oregano
	1 tsp	Basil
	1 tsp	Salt
	¼ tsp	White pepper
30 gm	⅓ cup	Green Coriander
	1 tbsp	Olive oil

For the sauce

	0.5 tsp	paprika
	0.5 tsp	salt
	⅓ cup	Green parsley

How to prepare:

Wash the fish and put it in a sever.

In a big container put the lemon juice, shredded skin of lemon, garlic, oregano, basil, water, white pepper, green coriander, and olive oil, stir well.

Put the fish in the mixture of soaking, cover it and keep it for next day inside the fridge.

Arrange the fish in an oven tray, cover it with aluminum foil, and bake it for almost 15 min. Remove the foil and broil it little from top to be golden color.

The sauce: Put the smashed garlic and chopped parsley, lemon juice, water and the salt with spices and mix them well. Then add them to the grilled fish. It goes with boiled rice or baked potato and salad.

Stuffed Mexican Squash

Category	Lunch
Serving	2 serving
Serving Size	2-3 pieces

Total kcal/ 1 serve 270 kcal

100 ml	Fresh Tomato juice
1 tsp	Tomato paste
0.5 tsp	Dry mint
2 gm	Sweet pepper

Cooking Items

500 gm	Mexican Squash
40 gm	Tomato
70 gm	Sushi Rice
50 gm	Meat
2 gm	Cinnamon
2 gm	Salt
2 gm	Black pepper
2 gm	Sweet pepper
2 gm	Basil spices
1 tsp	Coconut oil

For cooking the stuffed squash

0.5 tsp	Salt

For Covering the squash Water

3 Pc	Garlic

How to prepare:

Dig the squash. Mix the tomato for filling in the mixture. Put it in a container then add to it the meat, salt, cinnamon and sweet pepper, black pepper, basil spices the washed rice, and oil. Mix them well, then fill them inside the squash and arrange them in the saucepan, then put the squash in the pan and the water and salt of water and tomato paste, tomato juice and sweet pepper above them until the water covers the squash.

Put them on high fire until the boiling then on low fire and after 40 min add the smashed garlic and the dry mint and keep it until it cooked.

Okra Stew with Beef

Category	Lunch
Serving	7 serving
Serving Size	1 cup

Serving total kcal 200 kcal

Cooking Items	
1 kg	Okra (fresh)
1 kg	Tomato
300 gm	Onion
1 tbsp	Coconut Oil
2 tsp	Salt
1 tsp	Cardamon powder
25 gm	Garlic
¼ tsp	Cinnamon
¼ tsp	Black pepper
1 cup	Coriander(minced)
500 gm	Beef Meat(big cubes)

¼ cup	Lemon juice
1 cup	Water of meat How to prepare:

How to prepare:

Cut the onion into cubes, and boil the meat with cardamon and half the quantity of onion. Fry the onion and half quantity of garlic then add the boiled meat, the spices and the salt. Add the okra after washing it, stir, and keep it for 10 min on low fire.

Add the lemon juice and keep it 5 min.

Peel and cut the tomato and add to the okra and keep until it will be cooked for about 15 min.

Add then the smashed garlic and coriander to the okra.

Brown Rice with Shayria
(Angel Hair Spaghetti)

Category	Side lunch dish
Serving	3 serving
Serving Size	1 cup

Total kcal in 1 serve 135 kcal

Cooking Items

300 gm	1 cup	brown rice
45 gm		Shayria
10 ml	2 tsp	Coco nut oil
500 ml	2 cup	Water
3 gm	½ tsp	Salt
	1 tsp	Flax seeds
	1 tsp	Shea seeds
	0.5 tsp	Cinnamon
	0.5 tsp	Turmeric

How to prepare:

Soak the rice for 1 night in normal water.

Fry the shayria with the coconut oil until it become golden.

Add the water, salt, cinnamon, and turmeric.

When the water boils, add the rice and stir then cover the pan.

After 5 min, add the oil then keep it on very low fire from 20-30 min until it will be cooked.

Add the Shea seeds and flax seeds on top of it and serve it hot beside a protein and vegetable lunch.

Dinner

Stuffed Turkey

Category   Lunch/
Dinner
Serving   25 serving
Serving Size   ½ cup of
Rice + 130 gm of Turkey

Total breakfast calories
Total kcal is 375 kcal per 1
serving

Cooking Items

3.5 kg   Small turkey
60 gm   Garlic
60 gm   Green ginger
200 gm   Kiwi
2 tbsp   Tomato paste
1 tbsp   Chili paste
2 tbsp   Salt
1 tbsp   Paprika
1 tbsp   Black paper
2 tbsp   Olive oil
1 cup   Lemon juice

For the Rice filling

400 gm   Minced meat

1 tbsp   Salt
1 tbsp   cinnamon
1 tsp   Black pepper
3 cup   Sushi rice
1 cup   Chick peas
70 gm   Nuts for decoration
5 cup   Water

Wash and clean the turkey with water very well then dry it well with kitchen napkins. Smash the garlic and shred the kiwi after you peal it then add the green ginger that you pealed and shred it. After that, add the spices of turkey and the pastes, oil lemon juice, mix it well then marinate the turkey with the mixture with using turkey injection. Leave it for 24 hours at least. The next day, bake it on 450 F for 3 hours but every hour remove the excess water and put it back in the turkey to keep it juicy.

After the turkey is cooked, put the oven on broil to make it golden from top.

The Rice Preparation: Soak the rice when you put the turkey in the oven and after 2 hours, put the meat and the salt, cinnamon, black pepper, and stir it for 10 min. Add the rice and the boiled cooked chickpeas, then add the rice and the water. Keep it on high fire for 10 min then reduce the fire and cover the rice for 15 min to be cooked, then when the turkey is ready, put half quantity of the rice in it and the rest around it.

You can spread some raw or oven roasted nuts on top for decorating.

Keto Pizza with Meat

Category	Dinner
Serving	16 Serving
Serving Size	1 pc

Note: Kcal per serving 235

Cooking Items

100 gm	Green pepper
100 gm	Onion
100 gm	Tomato
1 tsp	Oregano
1 tsp	Salt
1 tsp	Black pepper
100 gm	Fresh mushroom
300 gm	Low fat mozzarella cheese
30 gm	Garlic
2 tbsp	Tomato paste
0.5 cup	Black olives
3 cup	Almond and oat Dough as the recipe of Almond Bread

300 gm	For the meat Lean beef minced meet
1 tsp	Cinnamon
1 tsp	Salt for the meat
1 tsp	Black pepper
1 tsp	Garlic powder

How to prepare:

Cut green pepper to long thin slices.

Cut tomato and onion into very small cubes and mushroom into 4 pc then into slices. Sauté the meat with its spices on medium fire and keep it aside.

Mix the tomato paste with the spices of the pizza and spread it on the almond dough and place all other vegetables, then the meat and bake it for 20 min at 450 F from down and when the dough is cooked add the cheese and put it on broil for 5 min.

Keep it to cool for 10 min and then slice it and serve it.

Healthy Grilled Beef Steak

Category	Dinner /Lunch
Serving	10 serving
Serving Size	100 gm

Total Serving calories 285 kcal
Total kcal/ 1slice = 285 kcal

Cooking Items

1 kg	Very lean Beef Steak
50 gm	Garlic
50 gm	Ginger
1 pc	Kiwi
1 tsp	Black pepper
1 tbsp	Olive oil
1 tsp	Paprika
1 tsp	Dried coriander
2 tsp	Salt

How to prepare:

Smash the garlic and shred the ginger and kiwi then mix all spices together. Marinate the meat, leave it for at least 3 hours.

Grill the steak in the Grill but try to put one of those grilling sheet under it to avoid the food poisoning by Carbon Dioxide. Grill it on one side to be cooked for 10 min then turn it upside down and leave it to be done for another 10 min.

Serve it with salad and 1 pc of grilled potato.

Green Fava Beans

Category	Dinner/Lunch
Serving	5 Serving
Serving Size	1 cup

Total breakfast calories   180 kcal/1 serve
Total kcal/ 180 kcal per 1 serve without the bread with it which is optional

Cooking Items

500 gm	Fava Beans
100 gm	Coriander
50 gm	Garlic
1 tbsp	Olive oil
5 gm	Paprika
10 gm	Salt
20 ml	Lemon Juice
0.5 tsp	Cinnamon
0.5 tsp	Black pepper

How to prepare:

Wash and cut the coriander, smash the garlic, sauté the green Fava Beans with olive oil over low fire then cover it. Leave it for 20 min. When it is cooked, add the coriander and the other spices with garlic and lemon juice.

Stir it and leave it for 2 minutes and close the fire. Let it cool for 10 min then serve it with 1 slice of whole bread + salad or yogurt.

Potato Wedges with Herps

Category	Carbs of Lunch or Dinner
Serving	5 Serving
Serving Size	1 cup
Total kcal/ 1 serve	130 kcal

Cooking Items

500 gm	Potato
1 tbsp	Olive oil
3 pc	Garlic
1 tbsp	Oregano
1 tbsp	Rosemary
1 tsp	Dry mint
1 tsp	Paprika
1 tsp	Cinnamon
7 gm	Salt

How to prepare:

Wash and peel the potato then cut it into long fingers. Put it in an oven tray, add the oil and spices, and mix it very well. Bake it from down for 15 min on 450 F then put it on broil from up for 1 to 2 min to gain some golden color then serve it with meat or chicken and vegetables.

Soy Meat Burger (Vegetarian)

Category	lunch
Serving size	3 serving
Serving/1 portion	⅓ cup
Total kcal/1 serving	300 kcal

Cooking Items

50gm	Soy meat
2 gm	Cinnamon
2 gm	Black pepper
2 gm	Mixed spices (seasoning spices with no salt)
40gm	brown bread (almond bread)
120gm (2pcs)	Potato for baking(potato wedges)
40gm	Flour
1tsp	Salt
½ pc	Egg white
¼ tsp	Salt and oregano for potato (seasoning salt)
40gm	Potato for soy meat

1Pc	Garlic
¼tsp	Glove grain
1tbsp	ketchup
1 tbsp	Mayonnaise light

Decoration Item for 1 serving

40gm	Lettuce (Ice berg)
60gm	Carrots (shredded)
50gm	White cabbage
3 slices	Cucumber pickles

How to prepare:

Soak soy meat overnight, chop it very fine, boil the potato of meat and peel it.

Blend it and add it to the meat, add smashed garlic, glove grain, cinnamon, black pepper, mixed spices flour, salt, egg white. Mix very well.

Brush oil on the try, make ⅓ cup of the meat round peace's and put it on the try. Then put it in oven until it will be cooked.

For Baking the Potato:

Peel potato and cut it into long slices, bring oven try and put aluminum foil and put on the potato, oil, and salt. Mix them. Cover them with aluminum foil and put it in oven.

AT RESTAURANT (extra saturated fat, bread with butter and milk, cheese, French fries may reach 700-1000 kcal sometimes)

Salad

Hala Hamza Seif

Spinach and Avocado Salad

Category	Salad
Serving	5 serving
Serving Size	1 cup
Total calories/serving	160
Total kcal/ 160 kcal	

How to prepare:

Wash the vegetable and arrange the spinach, broccoli, and carrot in the plate. Boil the eggs.

Smash the avocado and add the vinegar and the salt to make the avocado nice and creamy sauce. Add the slices of the onion and the pumpkin seeds and eggs.

Serve it with the avocado dressing.

Cooking Items

500 gm	Baby Spinach
100 gm	Slices of Carrot
100 gm	Slices of broccoli
100 gm	Onion
1 pc	Avocado
20 ml	Apple cider Vinegar
1 tsp	Salt
1 tbsp	Pumpkin Seeds
5 pc	Boiled egg

Green Salad with Tomato

Category	Salad
Serving	10 serving
Serving Size	1 ½ cup

Total kcal/ 1 serve 85 kcal

Cooking Items

5 Sticks	Spring Onion
2 Pound	Cucumber
2 Pound	Lettuce
1 cup	Cherry Tomato
1 tbsp	Dry mint
100 gm	White onion
100 ml	Lemon juice
1 tbsp	Salt
30 ml	Olive oil
0.5 cup	Fresh mint
1 cup	Parsley
2 tbsp	Pumpkin seeds
1 tbsp	Flax seeds

How to prepare:

Wash all the vegetables and cut small pieces.

Ground the flax seeds.

Squeeze the lemon, take out the juice and add salt and olive oil & pour it in the small sauce container.

Arrange the vegetables and then add the sauce, pumpkin seeds and flax seeds.

Then serve it.

Tabooleh

Category	Salad
Serving	5 serving
Serving Size	1 cup

Total kcal/ 1 serve 80 kcal

Note: Add ground Flax seeds 1 tsp to any salad

Cooking Items

	50 ml	Lemon juice
	½ tsp	Salt
	15 ml	Olive oil
250 gm	1 Big Bundle	parsley
	1 tsp	Dry Mint
	2 tbsp	Burgol/ Quinoa
	5 Stick/pecies	Green onion
	½ Small bundle	Fresh mint
700 gm	5 Big Pecies	Tomato

How to prepare:

Shopped parsley finely after you wash and dry it, and the tomato, onion and mint very small cubes and fine.

Mix them together. Add the 5 minutes soaked burgol (or 5 minutes boiled quinoa) and spices.

Mix the lemon and salt then add olive oil and mix all the ingredients together then add the grounded flax seeds on top.

Healthy Desserts

Mohalabia (Milk Pudding)

Category   Sweet
Serving   4 serving
Serving Size   1 cup

Total kcal/ 1 serve 125 kcal

Cooking Items

500 ml	Low fat milk
60 gm	Corn flour
1 tbsp	Rose water
1 tsp	Pistachio nut for decoration
5 tsp	Sorbitol

How to prepare:

Mix the milk with the corn flour and sorbitol then put it on medium fire and mix very well until become sticky and thick .

Then add the rose water mix for 5 min. and remove it and let it cool for 5 min then put in container for 1 cup,

Leave it cool then put on top of blended nuts and put it in the fridge till the time of serving.

Baklawa

Category	Light Snack
Serving	30 serving
Serving Size	30 pcs

Total kcal/ 1 serve 75 kcal / 1 serve (1 pc)

Cooking Items

1 Packet	Filo dough
2 cup	Walnut
1 tbsp	Rose water
0.5 cup	Coconut oil
0.5 cup	Sorbitol
1 tsp	Cinnamon

How to prepare:

Smash the walnuts nut then add the rose water and cinnamon.

Spread the half quantity of filo dough layes in the try then brush it with the melted coconut oil then add the mixture of walnuts then add the remaining layers with brushing it with the liquid coconut oil then cut it to oval shapes carefully and put it to bake in the oven at 450 F for 10-15 min.

When it is golden, add the sorbitol seryp and let it cool and serve it.

Cheese Halawa

Category	Sweet/breakfast/dinner
Serving	6 serving
Serving Size	2 pcs

Total kcal/ 1 serve 150 kcal

Cooking Items

200 gm	Low fat Mozzarella cheese
250 gm	Samolina
1 tbsp	Rose water
1 tbsp	Pistachio for decoration
0.5 cup	Light Rikota cheese
0.5 cup	Sorbitol
1 cup	Water

How to prepare:

Soak the mozzarella cheese to remove any salty taste from it for 3 hours. Mix all ingredients except the pistachio and the rikota cheese. Put the mixture on a low fire and keep stirring till the mixture become a rubbery dough. Roll the dough while it is hot and make a square with thickness of 0.5 cm then spread one line of rikota cheese (half amount) then roll it till the half then cut a row line and start another roll then cut the two rolls into small equal pieces and decorate it with pistachio.

Cookies of Dates

Category
Light Snack for diabetic and weight lose
Serving   20 pcs
Serving Size   1 pc

Total kcal for 1 serve 105 kcal

Cooking Items

2 cup	Wheat Flour (Gold blue)
3 tbsp	Anise spices
0.5 tsp	Cinnamon
1 gm	Salt
150 gm	Coconut oil/ or light butter
1 tsp	Yeast
40 ml	Rose water
0.5 cup	Stevia
100 ml	Water
350 gm	Dates
50 gm	Sesame

How to prepare:

Remove the seeds of dates and blend the dates very soft with the rose water.

Mix the dried things together (flour, anise spices, cinnamon, salt) then add the coconut oil and mix it well,then put in separate container the yeast water and stevia and leave it for 10 minutes then mix it with previous ingredients,and kneed very well. Let the dough take rest about 30 min.

Cut the dough into small balls thin fill it with 1 tsp of date paste then close it and roll it with sesame then form it as the shape that you like and you can keep it as balls.

Put in Oven on degree 400 F and the time of baking 5 to 10 min.

Remove it and let it to be cool then cover it with plastic.

Light Petit Four

Category	Dessert for diabetic and weight lose
Serving	60 serving
Serving Size	2 pcs combined together
Total kcal/ 1 serve 60 kcal	

For decorating

50 gm	Dark chocolate
50 gm	Strawberry jam
50 gm	Crashed pistachio
2 tbsp	Water

Cooking Items

1.5 cup	Coconut oil or light butter
2.5 cup	Wheat flour (Gold blue brand)
1.5 cup	Stevia sweetener
0.5 tsp	Vanilla
1 cup	Cacao powder /or flour if the cookies not a chocolate one
¼ tsp	Baking powder
1 Pc	Egg white

How to prepare:

Mix the egg white and the stevia sugar, butter, and vanilla, then add the flour and the cacao flour with baking powder. Put it in the cookies former and make it as small cookies.

Bake it for 5-6 minutes at 450 F.

Let the chocolate melt in a container over a pan of boiling water, then decorate the cookies with jam or chocolate syrup and nuts.

Basbusa / coconut cake

Category	Snack/dessert
Serving	20 serving
Serving Size	1 pc

Total kcal/ 1 70 kcal

Cooking Items

2 cups	Coconut powder
2 cups	Semolina
½ cup	Coco nut Oil
4pc	Egg white
1½ tbsp	Baking powder
2 cups	Low fat yogurt
200gms	Stevia sweetener
½ pc above every pc	Almond for decoration

How to prepare:

Heat the oven till 450 F. Mix the ingredients all together.

Put little butter in the baking try then put 1 tbsp. of flour and spread it all over the try then put the mixture, put it in side oven.

For 30 to 45 min, remove and leave it cold then cut it diamond shape, put almond for decoration.

Arabic Rolled Ice Cream

Category	Snack
Serving	30 serving
Serving Size	1 slice / ½ cup
Total kcal/ 1 serve	140 kcal

Cooking Items

3 cup	Light whip cream
1000 ml	Low fat Milk
1 cup	Stevia sugar
40 gm	Orchid /or Corn flour
3 gm	Mastic
1 tsp	Vanilla
1.5 cup	Water
2 tbsp	Pistachio powder for decoration

How to prepare:

Mix the milk and the orchid very well then put it on low fire and keep stirring till it becomes thick. Let it cool in the fridge for the next day.

In the second day, bring the thick milk mixture and add all the other ingredients except the pistachio, then mix it in the cake mixer for at least 10min.

Then freeze it for at least 15 hours. Remove it after and blend it well. Then lay a nonstick plastic in the tray and put the mixture in it. Arrange it to be equal and nice layer in the tray then cover it with plastic wrap and freeze it again.

Remove it after 10 to 15 hours at least and spread the pistachio or any other flavor you like and roll it after then freeze it for another 10 hours then cut it into slices and serve it.

Healthy Protein Bar

Category	Breakfast /Snack/Dinner
Serving	21 Serving
Serving Size	1 pc
Total kcal/ 1 serve	80 kcal

Cooking Items

1 cup	Sesame seeds
3 tbsp	Flax Seeds
3 tbsp	Chia Seeds
3 tbsp	Red Quinoa Seeds
3 tbsp	White Quinoa seeds
3 tbsp	Anise Seeds
2 cup	Oat Bran
1 tbsp	Cinnamon
1 cup	Honey
3 tbsp	Pumpkin Seeds
3 tbsp	Sunflower seeds

How to prepare:

Put the Sesame Seeds in a non-sticky pan and keep stirring on low fire till the sesame become golden. Add all other ingredients after that and mix it very well for 3 min. Then put it in a tray and press it with a flat spoon till become straight. Leave it to cool and cut it to small squares and serve it with green tea and mint as a healthy snack or with low fat milk as a breakfast or dinner.

Crunchy Kaak with Sesame

Category	Snack / breakfast with milk
Serving	30 serving
Serving Size	1 pc
Total kcal/ 1 serve	110 kcal

Cooking Items

4 cup	Whole grain flour
1.5 cup	Sugar powder/or Stevia sugar
200 gm	Coconut oil/or light butter
1 Pc	Egg
1 tsp	Corn flour
2 tbsp	Corn oil
2 tbsp	Baking powder
0.5 tsp	Soda carbonate
0.5 tsp	vanilla
2 tbsp	Anise spices
1 cup	Sesame seeds
1 tbsp	Black seeds
1 cup	Low fat milk

How to prepare:

Mix the dried ingredients together except the sesame and black seeds. Mix the liquid ingredients separately then add them together and mix for 5 min. After that, spread half quantity of the sesame and black seeds in the oven tray then put the dough in an icing bag and form it into 10 cm long sticks or round circles as the size of the hand palm. Then spread the remaining seeds on top and shake the tray to make sure that all dough are covered with the seeds. Then bake it o 400 F for 7 to 10 min and when it is golden remove it and let it cold. After an hour, serve it with tea or low fat milk or soymilk.

Kunafa with Milk Pudding

Category	Snack /breakfast
Serving	20 serving
Serving Size	1 pc
Total kcal/ 1 serve	135 kcal

Cooking Items

500 gm	Kunafa (very thin angle hair spaghetti)
1000 ml	Low fat Milk
0.5 cup	Stevia sugar
1 cup	Sorbitol
0.5 cup	Coconut oil or / light vegetarian butter
1 tsp	Vanilla
1 cup	Corn flour
2 tbsp	Pistachio powder for decoration

How to prepare:

1. Milk Pudding: Mix the milk, corn flour, stevia sugar, vanilla together and put it on low fire and keep stirring till the mixture be thick. Let it cool for 1 hour.

2. Mix the kunafa with coconut oil with your hands very well then spread half of it in the oven try and press it well, then add the cold pudding on top.

3. Put the other half of kunafa on top of the pudding and bake the tray for 5 to 10 min from down on 400 F.

4. Transfer the tray into another one upside down carefully, then bake it again for 5 min. to make it golden, then spread the sorbitol on top of it, and serve it.

Kunafa with Cheese (Samolina Sweet with Mozzarella cheese)

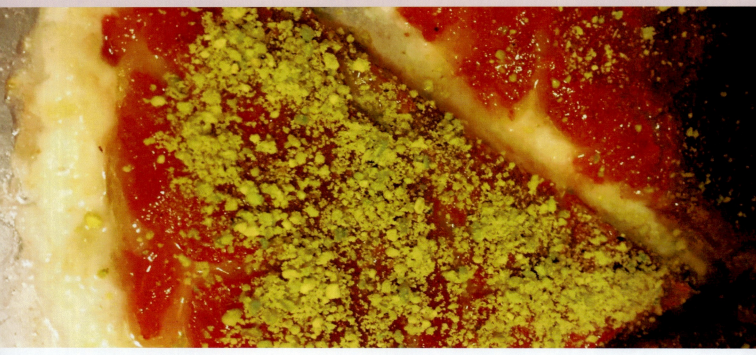

Category	Snack /breakfast
Serving	20 serving
Serving Size	1 pc
Total kcal/ 1 serve	130 kcal

Cooking Items

3 cup	Samolina
1 cup	All-purpose Flour
0.5 cup	Stevia sugar
1 cup	Sorbitol
1 cup	Low fat yoghurt
1 tbsp	Baking powder
1 tsp	Vanilla
30 ml	Corn oil
2 cup	Low fat Mozzarella cheese
2 cup	Water
2 tbsp	Pistachio powder for decoration

How to prepare: Mix all ingredients together except the sorbitol, Mozzarella cheese, pistachio. Then after mixing the dough very well it is going to be thicker that the texture of the cake little, bake it an 400 F for 20 min from down only then let it cool for 1 hour.

After that blend it to be very fine and in the oven try bruch it with nonstick oil and then spread the powder dough and press it well, then add the mozzarella cheese on top.

Bake the tray again from down only for around 5to 10 min then transfer it on another tray upside down and add the sorbitol and the pistachio then serve it warm as of the cheese should be melted.

Jello of Fruit Juice with Agar Agar

Category	Snack
Serving	6 serving
Serving Size	½ cup of juice + ½ cup of fresh fruits

Note: 120 kcal per serving

Cooking Items

900 gm	2 cup	Orange juice
250 gm	½ cup	Lemon juice
150 gm	½ cup	Strawberry juice
	1 tsp	Shredded Lemon and orange peel
8 gm	1 Stick	Agar Agar
60 gm	4 tbsp	Brown sugar or (Stevia sugar)
200 gm		Small Pieces of apple
250 gm		Pieces of Banana
80 gm		Pieces of strawberry
500 gm	2 cup	Water

How to prepare:

Soak the Agar for 1 hour in hot water.

Squeeze the fruits, and shred the skin of lemon and orange.

Put the agar on the colander and squeeze very well.

Then put this Agar liquid on the fire for 20 minutes.

Remove the agar liquid, add the juice and the sugar to it, and mix very well.

Cut the fruits small and arrange it in the deep plate then add the mixture of juice and agar.

Cover the plate with plastic wrap and put it in the fridge to cool and serve.

Maamool

Category	Snack
Serving	60 pcs
Serving Size	1 pc
Total kcal/ 1 serve	80 kcal

Cooking Items

2 cup	Flour. N1
½ cup	Semolina
1 cup	Coconut oil /light butter
1 tsp	Anise spices
1 tsp	Rose water
½ cup	Water
1 tsp	Baking powder
1 tsp	Vanilla
⅓ cup	Stevia /Brown Sugar

For Toppings

½ cup	Pistachio nut
½ cup	Coconut
1.5 tsp	Rose water
½ cup	Dates

4 tbsp	Water
2 tbsp	Stevia Sugar

How to prepare:

Dough: Put flour and semolina, baking powder, vanilla, anise spices, sugar, then add the oil, butter, and stir very well. Then knead with milk and rose water.

Leave it inside the fridge to take rest from the night until morning.

The Filling: Date: Remove the seeds and blend + ⅓ of rose water then make it balls in ¼ tsp.

Coconut: Put ½ cup of coconut + add ½ of the water, ⅓ of rose water + ½ of sugar of topping then make it balls in ¼ tsp.

Pistachio nut: Put ½ cup of pistachio nut then blend little + add ½ of the water, ⅓ of rose water + ½ of sugar of topping then make it balls and form it with cookies make. You can add sesame or pistachio on top for decoration.

Baking: 400 F from down for 7 to 10 min.

Printed in the United States
By Bookmasters